T0273121

Improving Regulatory Accountability

Robert W. Hahn
and
Robert E. Litan

American Enterprise Institute
for Public Policy Research
and
The Brookings Institution

1997

The research at the American Enterprise Institute was conducted as part of AEI's continuing program for the study of regulatory reform. The research at the Brookings Institution was conducted under the auspices of the Center for Law, Economics, and Politics. The research assistance of Jonathan Siskin and Fumie Yokota is gratefully acknowledged. We would also like to thank Arlene Holen, John Morrall, and Tom Walton for helpful comments.

To order call toll free 1-800-462-6420 or 1-717-794-3800. For all other inquiries please contact the AEI Press, 1150 Seventeenth Street, N.W., Washington, D.C. 20036 or call 1-800-862-5801.

ISBN 978-0-8447-7106-9
ISBN 0-8447-7106-6

1 3 5 7 9 10 8 6 4 2

Contents

Executive Summary

Although regulations resulting from legislative mandates often have no direct fiscal impact, they pose real costs to consumers as well as businesses. Regulations aimed at protecting health, safety, and the environment alone cost over $200 billion annually—about half as much as outlays for federal discretionary programs. Yet, the economic impacts of federal regulation receive much less scrutiny than discretionary programs in the budget.

In 1996 Senator Ted Stevens added an unprecedented amendment to the Omnibus Consolidated Appropriations Act of 1997 that could have a major impact on how regulations are assessed in the future. That amendment requires the director of the Office of Management and Budget to provide Congress with estimates of the total annual benefits and costs of federal regulatory programs and estimates of the benefits and costs of individual regulations. That is the first statute to mandate such an accounting.

The purpose of this primer is to lay out the case for such regular accounting beyond the steps mandated by the Stevens Amendment. In particular, we hope to enable policymakers to make better use of available economic tools as they develop more reliable and accessible information on the benefits and costs of regulations.

We conclude that the federal regulatory process is in need of repair. Part of what is required is an improved accounting statement conveying the benefits and costs of regu-

1

lation. The Office of Management and Budget, the Council of Economic Advisers, or both organizations should produce a unified economic regulatory accounting statement that systematically characterizes the benefits and costs of federal regulation on an annual basis in a form that would be accessible to a wide audience. The report would provide information to the public, interest groups, and legislators as they engage in debates about billion-dollar regulatory policies that are likely to affect all Americans.

While some will undoubtedly object to any proposal to reform regulation, we see our proposal as relatively modest. It does not require that regulations pass a benefit-cost or cost-effectiveness test. It simply helps to make an arcane, unsystematic process more transparent and systematic by introducing a unified approach for analyzing and disseminating key information on the effect that regulatory policies have on consumers, businesses, the environment, and government entities. The changes we propose will help promote democratic ideals by increasing public awareness and raising the accountability of our elected officials. They should also improve regulatory policies by developing more effective and less burdensome regulations.

1
Introduction

In 1996 Senator Ted Stevens added an unprecedented amendment on regulatory accountability to the Omnibus Consolidated Appropriations Act of 1997. The amendment, which may become the first step in a significant reform, deals not with spending but with federal regulations. It requires, for the first time, that the director of the Office of Management and Budget (OMB) provide Congress with "estimates of the total annual costs and benefits of Federal regulatory programs" and estimates of the benefits and costs of individual regulations.[1] That is the first statute to mandate an accounting of the benefits and costs of federal regulation. The amendment, attached to an annual appropriations bill, requires only one report, but Congress has expressed interest in receiving such a report on a regular basis.[2]

This primer lays out the case for such regular reports on the federal regulatory process and suggests some elements of the design and production of the reports. While that may on the surface appear to be merely a bookkeeping exercise, in practice it would have large, beneficial effects not only on the regulatory system itself but on the well-being of the nation as a whole.

Two factors have provoked the call for greater regulatory accountability: the unprecedented growth of federal regulatory activity since 1970—including environmental, health, and safety rules, employer mandates, and adminis-

3

trative paperwork burdens—and the increasing concern that the public is not getting its money's worth from regulation. Many scholars have shown that designing better rules could produce better regulatory results at a lower cost.[3]

To cite one example among hundreds of what that means, consider the case of Amoco's Yorktown, Virginia, refinery. The Environmental Protection Agency (EPA) required the Yorktown refinery to spend $31 million to reduce a small amount of benzene, when Amoco could have reduced five times as much for only $6 million had the agency afforded the firm more flexibility to comply with the rules.[4]

Although regulations resulting from legislative mandates often have no direct fiscal impact, they pose real costs to consumers as well as businesses. The Family and Medical Leave Act of 1993, for example, did not significantly affect federal spending, but the General Accounting Office (GAO) projected that the act would cost employers close to $700 million annually.[5] Regulations aimed at protecting health, safety, and the environment alone pose an annual cost of over $200 billion—about half as much as outlays for federal discretionary programs.[6] And according to the OMB, final regulations issued by federal executive agencies increased total costs to the economy by an average of $6 billion annually in real terms between 1987 and 1996.[7]

As efforts to balance the budget constrain programs involving spending, regulation will become an even more attractive tool for accomplishing social goals. The economic impact of regulation currently receives little scrutiny compared with the federal deficit. But as the public has become more aware of the inconsistency and waste in implementing various regulations, Congress has intensified its interest in more systematically measuring the economic impact of regulations. The aim is not to do away with regulations, nor, as some have charged, to halt the effort to reduce pollution or improve health and safety. Rather, it is to achieve the results at less cost and to curb regulations that impose huge costs with very little benefit.

The move toward a comprehensive accounting of regulatory impacts is a positive development because such a discipline will provide lawmakers with better information on which to design regulatory statutes and also make members of Congress more accountable to the public for regulations that are implemented in response to the laws they pass. While economic analysis should not replace political judgment in a democracy, it should inform the decision-making process and help encourage more effective and less wasteful regulation. Assessing the strengths and weaknesses of regulatory proposals can ensure a consistent, systematic measurement of the relevant benefits and costs across agencies.

Our purpose here is to provide guidelines for improving regulatory accountability beyond the steps mandated by the Stevens Amendment.[8] In particular, we hope to enable policymakers to make better use of available economic tools as they develop more reliable and accessible information on the benefits and costs of regulations.

Currently, the federal government does not systematically assess the effects of regulations. Although regulatory agencies analyze the impacts of some rules, they fail to assess the benefits and costs of many other regulatory activities.[9] Moreover, the quality and scope of the analysis vary dramatically across agencies and programs. Until recently, policymakers have made little effort to develop a systematic way of collecting information needed to evaluate the economic impacts of regulatory policies and actions. The 105th Congress should follow up the Stevens Amendment with a permanent reform.

2

Attempts to Assess the Benefits and Costs of Regulation

Scholars have increased their focus on the benefits and costs of federal and state regulation. Here, we highlight studies and databases that one can use to develop aggregate estimates of regulatory impacts based on analyses of specific regulations and programs.

The regulatory impact analysis (RIA), required initially by President Ronald Reagan's Executive Order 12291 and now by President Bill Clinton's Executive Order 12866, provides the primary source of information on the benefits and costs of each major regulation that an executive branch agency promulgates; independent agencies are not required to conduct such an analysis. Executive agencies generally perform the assessment for any regulation whose annual economic impact exceeds $100 million. Because executive agencies complete RIAs before regulations are put in place, RIAs provide rough estimates of the incremental economic benefits and costs of implementing different regulatory alternatives. In table 1 we offer an overview of the economic information contained in RIAs. The table includes regulations promulgated by the Consumer Product Safety Commission, the Mine Safety and Health Administration, the National Highway Traffic Safety Administration, the Occupational Health and Safety Administration, and the Environmental Protection Agency

TABLE 1
REGULATORY SCORE CARD, 1990 TO MID-1995

	All	Final	Proposed	CPSC	MSHA	NHTSA	OSHA-Health	OSHA-Safety	EPA
Number of regulations reviewed	92	58	34	1	1	6	9	5	70
Costs/savings assessed	99%	98%	100%	100%	100%	100%	100%	100%	99%
Benefits quantified[a]	87%	83%	94%	100%	100%	100%	100%	100%	83%
Health	55%	57%	53%	100%	100%	100%	100%	100%	41%
Pollution reduction	45%	41%	50%	0%	0%	0%	0%	0%	59%
Benefits monetized	25%	19%	35%	100%	0%	0%	0%	0%	31%
Agency finding that monetized benefits exceed costs	18%	16%	24%	100%	0%	17%	11%	20%	19%

NOTE: CPSC=Consumer Product Safety Commission; MSHA=Mine Safety and Health Administration; NHTSA=National Highway Traffic Safety Administration; OSHA=Occupational Safety and Health Administration; EPA=Environmental Protection Agency.

a. This category includes health benefits, benefits from pollution reduction, and any other benefits that were quantified or monetized.

SOURCE: Hahn (1996, 213, table 10-1).

from 1990 to mid-1995. In the table we show the number of regulations, the percentage of regulations for which the agency quantified some part of benefits and costs, and the fraction of regulations that would pass a benefit-cost test based on the agency's own dollar estimates.

The data in table 1 show the considerable variation in the type and quality of analysis that the executive branch agencies perform for individual regulations. While those agencies estimated some measure of costs for almost all regulations, the analyses of benefits were often incomplete. Moreover, the agencies could demonstrate that *quantified* monetary benefits would exceed quantified costs in less than 20 percent of all regulations promulgated. That does not imply, however, that less than one of five of the regulations would pass a benefit-cost test, because the agencies did not monetize many of the physical benefits, such as emission reductions. Nevertheless, more than half of those regulations appear not to have passed a benefit-cost test.[10]

In addition to the RIAs, executive agencies periodically survey areas related to regulation such as workplace injuries and expenditures on pollution abatement.[11] Although those surveys do not focus exclusively on regulatory costs, agencies have used them to assess the cost and effectiveness of different aspects of regulatory policy.

Executive agencies also occasionally issue reports that aggregate the costs of particular kinds of regulation or the benefits and costs of selected major regulations. Examples include the EPA's *Environmental Investments: The Cost of a Clean Environment*,[12] the National Highway Traffic Safety Administration and Federal Highway Administration's assessment of the impact of highway, traffic, and motor vehicle safety programs,[13] and the OMB's reports on the federal regulatory program.[14] *Until recently, however, there has been no effort to require the government to explore systematically the economic impacts of regulation.* Section 812 of the 1990 Clean Air Act Amendments does, however, require the EPA periodically to conduct a retrospective analysis of the benefits and costs of clean air regulations, as well as a prospective analysis every two years.

Scholars have also studied the aggregate benefits and costs of regulation and deregulation.[15] In addition, the Center for the Study of American Business at Washington University periodically reports on employment trends in regulatory agencies and the administrative costs associated with staffing those agencies.[16] The center does not, however, assess the economic impacts of the regulations that those agencies issue.

Recent legislation may change the haphazard approach to reporting and analyzing the benefits and costs of regulation. The Unfunded Mandates Reform Act of 1995,[17] the Small Business Regulatory Enforcement Fairness Act of 1996,[18] and the aforementioned regulatory accountability provision in the Omnibus Consolidated Appropriations Act of 1997 together provide a more systematic basis for informed decision making on regulatory impacts. We summarize the requirements of those laws as well as the mandates of Executive Order 12866 in table 2.

While the thrusts of each piece of legislation and the executive order differ, they share one common theme—a requirement that agencies use economic analysis to assess the benefits and costs of different kinds of regulations. The laws and executive order consider a range of impacts on different constituencies, such as small business, local governments, consumers, income groups, demographic groups, and the private sector. Not surprisingly, the laws and the executive order have considerable overlap. For example, the executive order requires the EPA to assess the benefits and costs of the 1986 amendments to the Safe Drinking Water Act because the annual economic impacts exceed $100 million, while the Unfunded Mandates Reform Act requires an assessment of the same law because the mandate on local governments exceeds $100 million annually.

The 104th Congress considered other bills addressing

TABLE 2
RECENT REGULATORY REFORM LEGISLATION AND EXECUTIVE ORDERS

Statute	Description
Unfunded Mandates Reform Act of 1995	CBO is required to estimate the costs of laws with new mandates in excess of $50 million in any one year on state, local, and tribal governments and in excess of $100 million in any one year on the private sector. Likewise, an executive branch agency must prepare a benefit-cost analysis of regulations with new mandates in excess of $100 million in any one year on state, local, and tribal governments or the private sector. The agency is required to choose the "least costly, most cost-effective, or least burdensome alternative" unless the provisions are inconsistent with law or the head of an agency can explain why such an alternative was not adopted.
Small Business Regulatory Enforcement Fairness Act of 1996[a]	An agency must submit each final regulation and the supporting analyses to Congress and the GAO. Congress has at least sixty calendar days to review major regulations before they can become effective. During that time, Congress can enact a joint resolution of disapproval that, if passed and then signed by the president, would void the regulation. In addition, strengthened judicial review provisions hold agencies more accountable for the impacts of regulation on small entities.

| Regulatory Accountability Provision of 1996[b] | By September 30, 1997, OMB must submit to Congress an assessment of the annual benefits and costs of all federal regulatory programs and of each rule with annual costs over $100 million. OMB can also make recommendations to reform or eliminate inefficient programs. |
| Executive Order 12866 (1993)[c] | An agency must submit to OMB's OIRA an assessment of the potential benefits and costs of significant regulatory actions. A more extensive benefit-cost analysis is required if a rule is considered "economically significant," as defined by one or more characteristics, such as an annual effect on the economy of $100 million or more or significant effects on productivity, competition, jobs, the environment, or public health or safety. |

a. This section of the act amends the Regulatory Flexibility Act of 1980.
b. This is the Stevens Amendment to the Omnibus Consolidated Appropriations Act of 1997.
c. This order contains requirements similar to those in Executive Order 12291 issued by President Reagan in 1981.

SOURCE: Hahn (1997b).

11

how agencies evaluate the benefits and costs of regulation. Although the House passed the Risk Assessment and Cost-Benefit Act in 1995, the Senate defeated its counterpart.[19] Major stumbling blocks included the bill's requirement that *all* health, safety, and environmental rules be subject to periodic review, benefit-cost mandates, and judicial review.

3
Guidance on Regulatory
Accounting Legislation

Although recent legislation will enhance regulatory accountability, further legislation is necessary. We propose legislation requiring the OMB, the Council of Economic Advisers (CEA), or a newly created independent agency to issue an annual or at least a biennial regulatory accounting report to Congress that outlines the regulatory activities of the federal government. The report should be written in an accessible format, comparable to the CEA's *Economic Report of the President,* and should be available on the Internet. The report should focus on the benefits and costs of regulation defined in terms of traditional economic measures of consumer and producer welfare.

Content of the Regulatory Accounting Report

Using those measures, the report should first and foremost provide a state-of-the-art review of the benefits and costs of federal regulation. Then the report should offer recommendations for reforms to promote more efficient regulations at a lower cost with less waste.

The state-of-the-art review should evolve over time. Initially, the organization producing the report should focus on developing data on the incremental benefits and costs of individual regulations that have recently been adopted.[20] It should use RIAs to estimate the economic impacts of major regulations promulgated by executive agencies. To assess the effects of *all* major regulations, our proposal would necessarily require the independent regulatory agencies to begin to conduct RIAs. Information derived from the RIAs would permit a crude estimate of the annual benefits and costs of regulation along with an assessment of their discounted present value.[21] Agencies should provide similar information for proposed regulations.

Eventually, the report should also include individual and aggregate estimates of the benefits and costs of past, present, and future regulations. Although aggregate estimates are less important initially because the best way to affect policy in the short term is to modify individual regulations, aggregate estimates do have value. They provide a better sense of areas in which the government has enhanced consumer welfare and economic efficiency, and they can help in developing a budget-like mechanism to encourage a more rational allocation of resources.[22]

The report should qualitatively describe important economic benefits and costs that are not easy to quantify. If, for example, a rule is likely to have an important positive impact on an ecosystem but its economic impacts are not easily measured, the report should describe the nature of those impacts as precisely as possible. Such descriptions enable voters to know what they are getting for their money.

Suggestions for reforms should include both procedural reforms to improve information and measurement and substantive reforms to improve the efficacy of regulation and to eliminate inefficient regulations. While reform is important, the organization producing the report should initially target its resources to develop state-of-the-art estimates of the benefits and costs of regulation so that those estimates can become central to the policy debate.

In addition to directly measuring consumer welfare and economic efficiency, the report should examine how regulation affects innovation, wages, employment, and income distribution—effects that are frequently very difficult to estimate. When such factors are particularly important, the reporting agency should assess their magnitude. The effects of regulation on employment should not, however, dominate the analysis, because they are extremely difficult to estimate. In addition, regulation rarely affects the overall level of employment, although it certainly can affect individual sectors.[23]

The organization producing the report should also use OMB data on paperwork to estimate the economic costs associated with administrative burdens on the private sector.[24] The report should not, however, present that category as a net cost of regulation without carefully analyzing alternative options for regulating with less paperwork. Since specifying such options is difficult, we prefer simply noting how paperwork requirements change over time and assigning a dollar value to the cost of such paperwork. Agencies could also use the format developed by the Center for the Study of American Business to report their administrative costs.[25]

Improving the Quality of RIAs

Agencies could dramatically improve the quality of RIAs by standardizing assumptions across analyses, providing a better treatment of uncertainties, defining baselines clearly, using peer-reviewed scholarship when available, and presenting results clearly.[26] In addition, agencies could use retrospective studies of actual impacts to complement prospective studies. Those analyses would provide a better assessment of actual benefits and costs and would improve prospective estimation techniques.

RIAs do not currently estimate the economic impacts of many regulatory activities. For example, agencies make almost no effort to compute the costs of licensing procedures, letters, minor regulations, and guidance.[27] Moreover, economic regulatory agencies do not typically estimate the potential gains from introducing greater competition into the markets that they regulate. Requiring the regulatory accounting report to include independent regulatory agencies, many of which are economic regulatory agencies, would increase the incentives of those agencies to consider the economic impacts of their regulatory activities.

The Role of Outside Parties

With a more transparent process and systematic accounting of the economic effects of regulations, outside parties should be in a position to help improve the quality of the estimates of regulatory impacts. The organization producing the regulatory accounting report should allow outside parties to submit comments on the substance of the document. That organization either could submit a preliminary version of the report for comment and briefly summarize comments in the final document or could publish that summary in the subsequent report.

Production of the Report

Report Producer. Either the OMB or the CEA would be the appropriate organization to produce the report. Both organizations have excellent reputations for their technical economic expertise. Each has its advantages: the OMB has a larger staff and more familiarity with details of regulation; the CEA is more closely aligned with the goal of promoting economic efficiency—ensuring that the public gets full value for its money—than is the OMB, with its preoccupation with balancing the budget. Perhaps the two organizations could collaborate. The leaders of those organizations should sign a statement on the front page of the document to certify that the estimates contained therein represent the best collective wisdom of their economists on the benefits and costs of regulation.

An alternative to choosing the OMB, the CEA, or both to produce the report would be to set up an independent agency charged with that function. A call for creating such an agency is premature without first using one or both of those established organizations, but creating a new independent agency might be a viable option later.

Frequency. Ideally, the government should issue the report annually to facilitate analyzing and improving the steady flow of regulations costing billions of dollars per year. The information to produce the report already exists and will improve over time.

Data Production, Data Analysis, and Final Reporting. Production of the report would entail three stages: data production, data analysis, and final reporting. Responsibilities for the first two stages would evolve over time. Initially, the agency promulgating a regulation should produce the raw data on the benefits and costs of that regulation. Ultimately, that first stage would be subject to oversight by the organization producing the report to limit possible bias. In the second stage, the agency promulgating a regulation and the organization producing the report would share the responsibility for analyzing the raw data. In the short term, the agency producing the raw data would play a greater role in analyzing the data. In the long term, the organization producing the report should develop enough independent expertise to have primary responsibility for the analysis. Moving the primary responsibility for analyzing the data to the organization producing the report should improve the quality of the estimates because regulatory agencies are more likely to use inconsistent accounting measures and to choose those measures that favor their particular programs.

Resource Needs

The additional resources required for the analytical efforts we are proposing would be minuscule compared with the costs that regulations impose. The executive agencies already bear the costs of producing the RIAs; the independent agencies would have to undertake RIAs, and that would entail an additional cost. As we noted, the methods used to produce RIAs are not standardized across—and sometimes even within—agencies, so there would be a one-time cost associated with developing and implementing standard estimating and reporting methods. In addition, the organization producing the report would bear some costs in helping to refine the RIAs, but the OMB already performs that task in its oversight activities. Accordingly, the main additional costs would be associated with conducting RIAs for the independent agencies and with assembling and then analyzing the relevant data found in all RIAs for the major rules.[28]

We estimate that ten full-time-equivalent senior economists or analysts could carry out those tasks, which would cost approximately an additional $1 million annually. Even if expenses for administration, outside contractors, and printing doubled or trebled that cost, the resulting total of several million dollars a year would pale compared with the overall annual cost of regulation. Moreover, the process of making regulatory activity much more transparent should produce savings of regulatory costs that would easily outweigh the additional costs associated with the enhanced accountability.

In fact, the U.S. government currently allocates very few resources for producing and reviewing RIAs. An average home buyer spends more, as a proportion of the cost of the house, for a general house inspection than the government spends on analyzing regulations.[29] Just as home buyers need to know whether they are getting good value for their money, so do the beneficiaries of new regulations.

Another perspective on the problem of accurate regulatory accounting comes from the number of civil servants working on regulations compared with the number reviewing their economic content. While more than 130,000 full-time-equivalent employees work at federal regulatory agencies, OMB's Office of Information and Regulatory Affairs (OIRA) has only forty-two professionals, fewer than half of whom actually review the economic analysis in the RIAs.[30]

Accessibility of the Report

The report should be presented in a clear, user-friendly format that is available on the Internet. One of the problems with existing regulatory impact analyses is that they are very difficult to read and vary widely in quality. The report should be accessible to a wide audience. A good model for the style and clarity of the report is the CEA's *Economic Report of the President.*

4

Responding to the Critics

Economists may value benefit-cost analysis more highly than others do. While this primer is not the place to provide a comprehensive defense of benefit-cost analysis, it is worthwhile to examine criticisms of the regulatory accounting tool that we are proposing. Four criticisms that we consider are workability, potential delay, potential to overemphasize costs at the expense of benefits, and the absence of any impact on policy.

Critics of improved accounting often argue that such measures are unworkable. They correctly point out the potential to misuse the instrument. That is true of almost any analytical approach, however. The critics must address the question of whether such analysis is preferable to the current regulatory mode, in which decisions tend to be driven more by inaccurate, incomplete, and inconsistently measured information. Surely, the status quo needs improvement.

Critics frequently contend that requirements for more economic analysis of regulations can cause "paralysis by analysis"—delaying the policy process. Simply requiring an agency to provide a systematic regulatory accounting need not delay implementing a specific regulation. Moreover, should a regulatory accounting statement cause policymakers to rethink regulatory priorities, that could be a good outcome, even if there were a delay. Policymakers could exempt emergency rulemaking from certain procedural requirements but not from the requirement that, to the extent practicable, their benefits and costs be included in the regular report.

Critics of benefit-cost analysis also assert that it focuses on those factors that can be quantified and tends to give short shrift to those factors that cannot be easily quantified. Those critics contend that benefits, which may be less easy to quantify than costs, will get short shrift. But a regulatory accounting requirement will, if anything, push the reporting organization and the regulatory agencies to improve their measurements of benefits. That is our reason for recommending that the regulatory accounting report highlight qualitative economic impacts where they are thought to be important.

Finally, some scholars have criticized calls for more comprehensive regulatory accounting because the existing system of regulatory oversight already imposes analytical requirements that appear to make little difference. We assert, however, that improved analysis and dissemination of information on the impacts of regulation can help weed out ineffective and wasteful regulations and improve regulations that are implemented, as Congress and the executive branch become better informed about how regulations require the allocation of scarce consumer and taxpayer dollars. That change will come in part from the information itself, which heretofore has not been readily accessible. Putting all regulatory information in one place will facilitate comparisons of the effect of individual rules and thereby assist Congress, the regulatory agencies, and the White House to think more seriously about how to set regulatory priorities and design better regulations.

5

Conclusions

The federal regulatory process is in need of repair. Part of what is required is an improved accounting statement conveying the benefits and costs of regulation. This primer has identified key elements in that accounting statement.

Improved regulatory accounting is not a panacea, but it is a step in the right direction.[31] The OMB, the CEA, or both organizations can usefully produce a unified economic regulatory accounting statement that systematically characterizes the benefits and costs of federal regulation on an annual basis in a form that will be accessible to a wide audience. The report will provide information to the public, interest groups, and legislators as they engage in debates about billion-dollar regulatory policies that are likely to affect all Americans.

While some will undoubtedly object to any proposal to reform regulation, we see our proposal as relatively modest. It does not require that regulations pass a benefit-cost or cost-effectiveness test. It simply helps to make an arcane, unsystematic process more transparent and systematic by introducing a unified approach for analyzing and disseminating key information on the effect that regulatory policies have on consumers, businesses, the environment, and government entities. The changes we propose will help promote democratic ideals by increasing public awareness and raising the accountability of our elected officials. They should also improve regulatory decision making.

The regulatory reform debate has become unnecessarily polarized. Congress now has a unique opportunity to reduce the rhetoric and substantively improve policymaking by asking government agencies to lead an effort to characterize systematically the impact of all federal regulation. The public has a right to know about those regulatory impacts. Just as every American business must gather and present its economic and accounting information in an organized manner, so must regulatory agencies gather and organize pertinent information on the benefits and costs of regulations in an intelligible, systematic way. Only then will the American people begin to gain a better sense of what they are getting in return for their investment in different kinds of regulation.

Notes

1. Omnibus Consolidated Appropriations Act of 1997, U.S. Public Law 104-208, sec. 645, 1996 U.S.C.C.A.N. (110 Stat. 3009): 1088–89.

2. See, for example, Thompson (1997).

3. See, for example, Anderson et al. (forthcoming), Tengs and Graham (1996), Morrall (1986), and Viscusi (1996).

4. See Amoco Corporation and U.S. Environmental Protection Agency (1992).

5. See General Accounting Office (1993).

6. See Hopkins (1992) and Office of Management and Budget (1997).

7. See Office of Management and Budget, Office of Information and Regulatory Affairs (1997).

8. "Regulatory accounting" refers to a requirement for the executive branch to report the impact of regulation in terms of its economic benefits and costs. "Regulatory accountability" is a broader concept aimed at making legislators and regulators more accountable for regulation. We believe that a good regulatory accounting statement will help promote regulatory accountability, but so too will other policies. See Crandall et al. (1997).

9. See Furchtgott-Roth (1996) and Hahn (1996).

10. See Hahn (1996, 218). To make the analysis consistent across different programs and regulations, Hahn converted estimates to 1994 dollars and used common discount rates and values for reducing health risks.

11. See, for example, the U.S. Department of Labor, Bureau of Labor Statistics's annual *Workplace Injuries and Illnesses.*

12. See Environmental Protection Agency (1990).

13. See National Highway Traffic Safety Administration and Federal Highway Administration (1991).

14. See Office of Management and Budget (1993).

15. See, for example, Weidenbaum and DeFina (1978), Litan and

25

Nordhaus (1983), Hahn and Hird (1991), Hopkins (1992), Winston (1993), Hahn (1996), Winston (1997), and Guasch and Hahn (1997). Although occasionally updated and expanded, those studies are generally not done on any regular basis.

16. See, for example, Warren and Jones (1995).

17. Public Law 104-4, March 22, 1995, 109 Stat. 48.

18. Public Law 104-121, Title II, March 29, 1996, 110 Stat. 857-874.

19. See H.R. 1022, 104th Congress, First Session, Risk Assessment and Cost-Benefit Act of 1995; S. 343, 104th Congress, First Session, Comprehensive Regulatory Reform Act of 1995; and S. 291, 104th Congress, First Session, Regulatory Reform Act of 1995.

20. Where estimates of aggregate regulatory impacts are available or can easily be estimated, they should be reported, but they should not be the primary focus at the outset.

21. The present value is computed by applying a discount factor to the annual benefits and costs, which takes into account the tradeoff between present and future consumption.

22. See, for example, Crandall et al. (1997) and Litan and Nordhaus (1983).

23. See, for example, Arrow et al. (1996).

24. See Office of Management and Budget (1996a).

25. See Warren and Jones (1995).

26. For more detailed discussions of those improvements, see Arrow et al. (1996), Hahn (1996), and the Office of Management and Budget (1996b).

27. See, for example, Huber and Thorne (1997), Furchtgott-Roth (1996), and Hahn (1997a).

28. It is difficult to estimate the resources that independent agencies would require to provide the necessary information for a regulatory accounting statement because relatively little is known about the economic impacts of agencies' rules, licensing requirements, and other activities. Nonetheless, those agencies frequently collect data on the economic implications of some of their activities, and their economists and policy analysts could help to develop RIAs. Thus, we believe that the additional resources needed would be modest, given a suitable reallocation of agency resources.

29. A review of executive agency RIAs from 1990 to mid-1995 showed that the average present value of gross costs for fifty-four final regulations was $5.1 billion in 1995 dollars (Hahn 1996). In a review of eighty-five RIAs, the Congressional Budget Office found that the average cost was $570,000 in 1995 dollars, which is .01 percent of the average cost of the regulation (Congressional Budget Office 1997). In contrast, for a single home valued at $200,000, a prospective homeowner spends $200 to $250 for a general house inspection, incurring a cost that is approxi-

mately .1 percent of the price of the home (based on the authors' telephone survey of Washington, D.C., home inspectors). Thus, a home buyer spends about ten times more than the government when assessing a prospective investment.

30. The full-time equivalent employment at federal regulatory agencies comes from Warren and Jones (1995). OIRA staff numbers come from the *Federal Staff Directory, Spring-1997* (1997). While twenty-four of the OIRA professionals review the relevant regulatory agencies, they devote a significant amount of their time to ensuring compliance with information collection requirements under the Paperwork Reduction Act of 1980.

31. In particular, we believe that improved regulatory accounting could form the basis for applying other techniques aimed at developing smarter regulation, such as a regulatory budget. See Crandall et al. (1997). We hasten to add, however, that a systematic accounting of regulation is worth doing for its own sake because of the positive impact it is likely to have on the regulatory process and the design of regulations.

References

Amoco Corporation and U.S. Environmental Protection Agency. 1992. *Amoco/U.S. EPA Pollution Prevention Project: Project Summary.* Chicago.

Anderson, Robert, Alan Carlin, Al McGartland, and Jennifer Weinberger. Forthcoming. "Cost Savings from the Use of Market Incentives for Pollution Control." In *Market-Based Approaches to Environmental Policy*, ed. Richard Kosobud and Jennifer Zimmerman. New York: Van Nostrand Reinhold.

Arrow, Kenneth J., Maureen L. Cropper, George C. Eads, Robert W. Hahn, Lester B. Lave, Roger G. Noll, Paul R. Portney, Milton Russell, Richard Schmalensee, V. Kerry Smith, and Robert N. Stavins. 1996. *Benefit-Cost Analysis in Environmental, Health, and Safety Regulation: A Statement of Principles*, Washington, D.C.: AEI Press.

Congressional Budget Office. 1997. *Regulatory Impact Analysis: Costs at Selected Agencies and Implications for the Legislative Process.* Washington, D.C.: Congressional Budget Office.

Council of Economic Advisers. Annual. *Economic Report of the President.* Washington, D.C.: Government Printing Office.

Crandall, Robert W., Christopher DeMuth, Robert W. Hahn, Robert E. Litan, Pietro S. Nivola, and Paul R. Portney. 1997. *An Agenda for Federal Regulatory Reform.* Washington, D.C.: AEI Press and Brookings Institution Press.

Environmental Protection Agency. 1990. *Environmental Investments: The Cost of a Clean Environment.* Report of the Administrator of the Environmental Protection Agency to the Congress of the United States, EPA-230-11-90-083. Washington, D.C.: Government Printing Office.

Furchtgott-Roth, Harold. 1996. "Neglect of Costs in Federal Regulation: Benign or Malignant?" Paper presented at conference, Regulatory Reform: Making Costs Count, December 9, at American Enterprise Institute, Washington, D.C.

General Accounting Office. 1993. "Family and Medical Leave Cost Estimate." GAO/HRD-93-14R. Washington, D.C.: Government Printing Office.

Guasch, J. Luis, and Robert W. Hahn. 1997. "The Costs and Benefits of Regulation: Implications for Developing Countries." Policy Research Working Paper 1773 and background paper for the *World Development Report 1997.* Washington, D.C.: World Bank.

Hahn, Robert W. 1996. "Regulatory Reform: What Do the Government's Numbers Tell Us?" In *Risks, Costs, and Lives Saved: Getting Better Results from Regulation,* ed. Robert W. Hahn. New York and Washington, D.C.: Oxford University Press and AEI Press.

———. 1997a. "Regulatory Reform: Assessing the Government's Numbers." In *Reviving Regulatory Reform,* ed. Robert W. Hahn. New York and Washington, D.C.: Cambridge University Press and AEI Press. Forthcoming.

———. 1997b. "Regulation and Its Reform around the World." In *Reviving Regulatory Reform,* ed. Robert W.

Hahn. New York and Washington, D.C.: Cambridge University Press and AEI Press. Forthcoming.

Hahn, Robert W., and John A. Hird. 1991. "The Benefits and Costs of Regulation: Review and Synthesis." *Yale Journal on Regulation* 8: 233–78.

Hopkins, Thomas D. 1992. "Costs of Regulation: Filling the Gaps." Report prepared for Regulatory Information Center. Washington, D.C.

Huber, Peter W., and John Thorne. 1997. "Economic Licensing Reform." In *Reviving Regulatory Reform*, ed. Robert W. Hahn. New York and Washington, D.C.: Cambridge University Press and AEI Press. Forthcoming.

Litan, Robert E., and William D. Nordhaus. 1983. *Reforming Federal Regulation*. New Haven: Yale University Press.

Morrall, John F. 1986. "A Review of the Record." *Regulation* 10 (November/December): 25–34.

National Highway Traffic Safety Administration and Federal Highway Administration. 1991. *Moving America More Safely: An Analysis of the Risks of Highway Travel and the Benefits of Federal Highway, Traffic, and Motor Vehicle Safety Programs*. Washington, D.C.: Government Printing Office.

Office of Management and Budget. 1993. *Regulatory Program of the United States Government*. Washington, D.C.: Government Printing Office.

———. 1996a. *Information Resources Management Plan of the Federal Government*. Washington, D.C.: Government Printing Office.

———. 1996b. "OMB Document on 'Best Practices' for Preparing Economic Analysis of Regulatory Action." Washington, D.C.: Bureau of National Affairs.

———. 1997. *Budget of the United States: Historical Tables*. Washington, D.C.: Government Printing Office.

Office of Management and Budget, Office of Information and Regulatory Affairs. 1996. *More Benefits, Fewer Burdens: Creating A Regulatory System That Works for the American People.* Report to the President on the Third Anniversary of Executive Order 12866. Washington, D.C.: Government Printing Office.

Omnibus Consolidated Appropriations Act of 1997. U.S. Public Law 104-208, sec. 645, 1996 U.S.C.C.A.N. (110 Stat. 3009): 1088–89.

Tengs, Tammy O., and John D. Graham. 1996. "The Opportunity Costs of Haphazard Social Investments in Life-Saving." In *Risks, Costs, and Lives Saved: Getting Better Results from Regulation*, ed. Robert W. Hahn. New York and Washington, D.C.: Oxford University Press and AEI Press.

Thompson, Fred. 1997. "Regulatory Burden Must Be Reformed." Remarks before the U.S. Chamber of Commerce, April 27, Washington, D.C.

U.S. Department of Labor, Bureau of Labor Statistics. Annual. *Workplace Injuries and Illnesses.* Washington, D.C.: Government Printing Office.

Viscusi, W. Kip. 1996. "The Dangers of Unbounded Commitments to Regulate Risk." In *Risks, Costs, and Lives Saved: Getting Better Results from Regulation*, ed. Robert W. Hahn. New York and Washington, D.C.: Oxford University Press and AEI Press.

Walker, P. Wayne, ed. 1997. *Federal Staff Directory, 1997-Spring.* 24th ed. Washington, D.C.: C Q Staff.

Warren, Melinda, and Barry Jones. 1995. "Reinventing the Regulatory System: No Downsizing in Administration Plan." Occasional Paper 155, Center for the Study of American Business, Washington University.

Weidenbaum, Murray, and Robert DeFina. 1978. *The Cost of Federal Regulation of Economic Activity.* American Enterprise Institute Reprint No. 88. Washington, D.C.: American Enterprise Institute.

Winston, Clifford. 1993. "Economic Deregulation: Days of Reckoning for Microeconomists." *Journal of Economic Literature* 31: 1263–89.

———. 1997. "U.S. Industry Adjustment to Economic Deregulation." *Journal of Economic Perspectives* 11. Forthcoming.

About the Authors

Robert W. Hahn is a resident scholar at the American Enterprise Institute, a research associate at Harvard University, and an adjunct professor of economics at Carnegie Mellon University. Before that he worked for two years as a senior staff member of the President's Council of Economic Advisers. Mr. Hahn frequently contributes to general-interest periodicals and leading scholarly journals including the *New York Times*, the *Wall Street Journal*, the *American Economic Review*, and the *Yale Law Journal*. In addition, he is a cofounder of the Community Preparatory School—an inner-city middle school that provides opportunities for disadvantaged youth to achieve their full potential. Mr. Hahn's current research interests include the reform of regulation in developed and developing countries and the design of new institutions for reforming regulation.

Robert E. Litan is director of the Economic Studies Program at the Brookings Institution. Formerly, he served as associate director of the Office of Management and Budget, as deputy assistant attorney general in the Antitrust Division of the Department of Justice, and as a regulatory specialist for the President's Council of Economic Advisers. An economist and an attorney who has practiced law and taught banking law at the Yale Law School, Mr. Litan has authored or coauthored numerous books and articles on financial institutions, international trade, and regulatory issues. His first book, *Reforming Federal Regulation*, co-authored with William D. Nordhaus (Yale University Press, 1983), anticipated many of the issues that are raised in this primer.